Learn How to play the right way

ASAP

BEGINNING
4-STRING BASS
METHOD
BY BRIAN EMMEL

ISBN 978-1-57424-385-7
SAN 683-8022

Cover by James Creative Group

Cover photos (l to r): Barry Bass of Phony Ppl; Scott Harris of Robert Plant & The Sensational Space Shifters; Jerry Wonda.

Bass Guitar and artist photos on the cover courtesy of D'Angelico Guitars.

Copyright © 2019 CENTERSTREAM Publishing
P.O. Box 17878 - Anaheim Hills, CA 92817

www.centerstream-usa.com | centerstrm@aol.com | 714-779-9390

Contents

How To Use This Book

This book is designed to teach you correctly how to sight-read and at the same time acquire a musical vocabulary with the associated terms. Also designed in the open to the fourth position studies (open notes, 1st, 2nd, 3rd, & 4th fret notes). The exercises contained in this book are presented in a progressive format; it starts out very easy and gets progressively harder improving your bass playing skills as you work through the book

The main points in this book

1st-4th STRING STUDIES:

This section will teaches you through a progressive method of learning notes and rhythm, one string at a time. Each page introduces new rhythm exercises. Each exercise gets progressively harder. Go as far as you can on each single string exercise. You may consider a bass guitar private instructor to help you.

THE RHYTHM GALLERY:

This exercise room is designed to warm you up to rhythm notation. If, you find yourself getting frustrated with the following chapters, go back to the Rhythm Gallery and hang out.

ENHARMONIC STUDIES:

These exercises introduce sharps, flats and naturals in the position studies.

CHORDS AND ARPEGGIOS:

The chord study exercises are laid out to develop your sight-reading and chord construction knowledge over different time signatures. This section of the book covers ALL the keys.

BLUES PROGRESSIONS:

This section puts you in a playing situation; it pulls all the previous studies together and allows you to interact with other instrument players. Again, I recommend a music teacher to help you interact in learning to play with other musicians and drummers.

CHORD CHARTS:

This is the last chapter; it allows you to improvise over the chord exchanges, using the knowledge gained from the chord studies chapter.

General Information

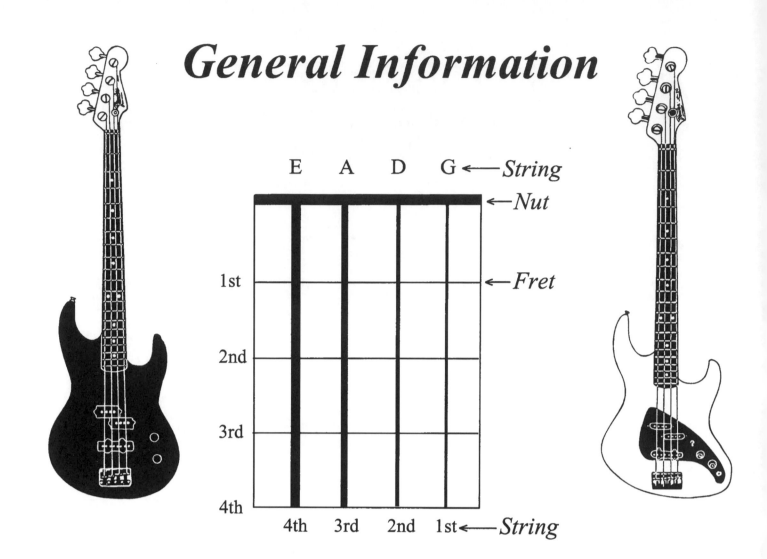

E   A   D   G ← *String*

← *Nut*

1st ← *Fret*

2nd

3rd

4th

4th   3rd   2nd   1st ← *String*

Left Hand Rules

Fingers 1-4 will be assigned to each four fret study position. For example; the first position of study will be on frets 1-4, and include all open notes, therefore: finger #1 will be assigned to fret # 1, finger #2 to fret #2, finger #3 to fret #3, and finger #4 to fret #4.

Right Hand Rules

You will be using a two finger alternating technique, which employs the index finger(i) and the middle finger(m). The alternating technique is much like walking, always exchanging fingers with each note played.

4

Method of String Tuning

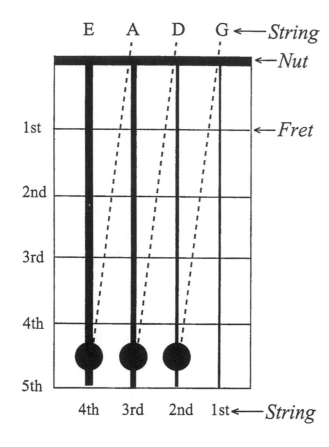

E   A   D   G ←—String

4 EASY STEPS TO GETTING IN TUNE

1. Tune the 4th string to the piano E note (19th white key from left), or purchase a pitch pipe for guitar at a local music store.
2. Place 1st or 2nd finger of left hand behind the 5th fret of the 4th string (play), this will give you the pitch of the 3rd string (open) A note (tune).
3. Repeat step 2 on 5th fret of 3rd string to (open) D note (tune).
4. Repeat on 5th fret of 2nd string to (open) G note (tune).

FINDING NOTES BY OCTAVE

An Octave is a tone (note) on the eighth degree of a given tone (note). This is determined by a standard musical SCALE: **DO-RE-ME-FAH-SOL-LA-TI-DO**

        1   2   3   4   5   6 7 8

The diagram below illustrates individual notes and their related octave. Finding notes by an **octave pattern** is the easiest way to learn notes. Simply start with the E note on the 4th string, move up **ONE WHOLE STEP** (2 frets) and skip over the 3rd string to the 2nd string's 2nd fret. Now go the the 3rd string's 7th fret E note, move up **ONE WHOLE STEP** (2 frets), to the 1st string's 9th fret, and there's it's octave E note. Finally you'll notice that the process repeats all over at the 12th fret, which is the similar to the **NUT** position.

The **DOTS** on the fret board indicate all the **ODD** numbered frets to help you locate.

The best way to learn notes is by **OCTAVE** and by taking one note name at a time. For example, learn all the E notes and then the F notes, F#/Gb's, G's, etc....

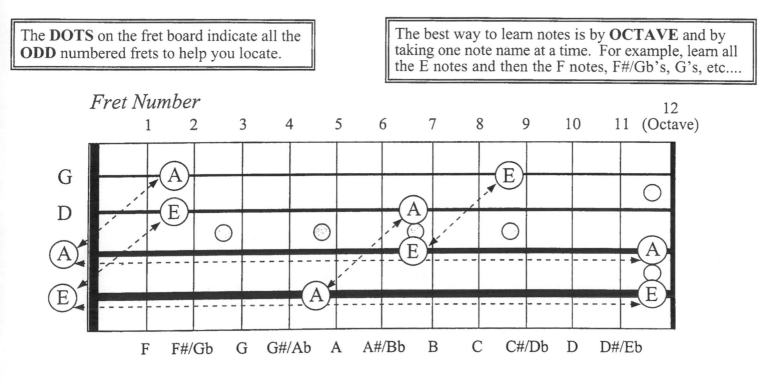

5

Music Symbols

STAFF

Music notation is written on a **STAFF**. A staff has 5 lines and 4 spaces. Notes are written on the staff to determine the **PITCH**(highness and lowness). The higher on the staff the note is written the higher the sound(pitch) of the note(s), and vice versa the lower. This is called the note **REGISTER.**

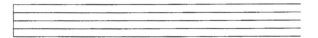

At the beginning of the staff is the **CLEF** sign. This symbol tells you that the music is notated for a bass instrument to play.

Each **LINE** and **SPACE** on the staff have letter names.
Lines below and above the staff are called **LEDGER LINES.**

Register

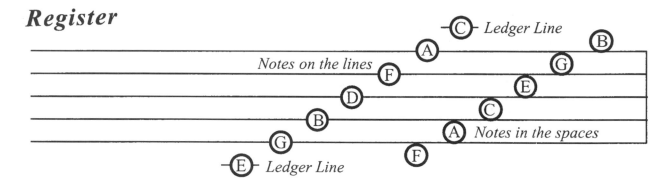

Another symbol to become familiar with is the **BAR LINE**. The bar line divides the beats of music and groups these beats into **MEASURES** for reading music over **TIME** and **TEMPO**(speed). A **DOUBLE BAR LINE** is used to show that it is the end of the piece or a particular section of the piece.

THE REPEAT SIGN
1ST AND 2ND ENDING SYMBOLS

The **REPEAT** sign means to repeat the song, or to go back to the nearest **REPEAT** sign and play from that section of the song forward.

1ST ENDING means to play that bar or measure the first time through, skip it and play the **2ND ENDING** on the second pass through the song.

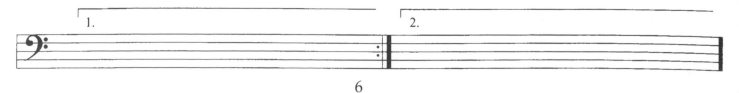

Time Signatures

There are basically two types of **TIME** fractions in music, **SIMPLE**(beats divisible by 2), and **COMPOUND**(beats divisible by 3). In this book we will work with 4/4 and 3/4 time. The top number indicates the number of beats per measure. The bottom number indicates what type of note receives one beat.

   **FOUR BEATS PER MEASURE**

THE QUARTER NOTE GETS ONE BEAT

   **THREE BEATS PER MEASURE**

THE QUARTER NOTE GETS ONE BEAT

Notes and Their Values

We will be using four different note types throughout this book.

Whole Note

1 2 3 4

Half Note

1 2   3 4

Quarter Note

1   2   3   4

Eight Note

1 & 2 & 3 & 4 &

Rest Symbols

Each note type has a related **REST** value or beats of silence.

Whole Rest

4 Beats

Half Rest

2 Beats

Quarter Rest

1 Beat

Eighth Rest

1/2 Beat

Summary:
Notes and Related Rests

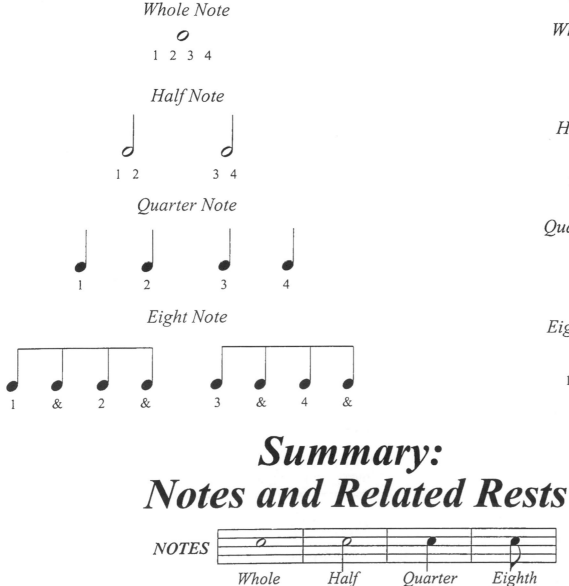

	Whole 4 counts	Half 2 counts	Quarter 1 count	Eighth 1/2 count
NOTES				
RESTS	1 2 3 4	1 2	1	1/2

1st String Studies
G String Exercise (Notes G, A, and B)

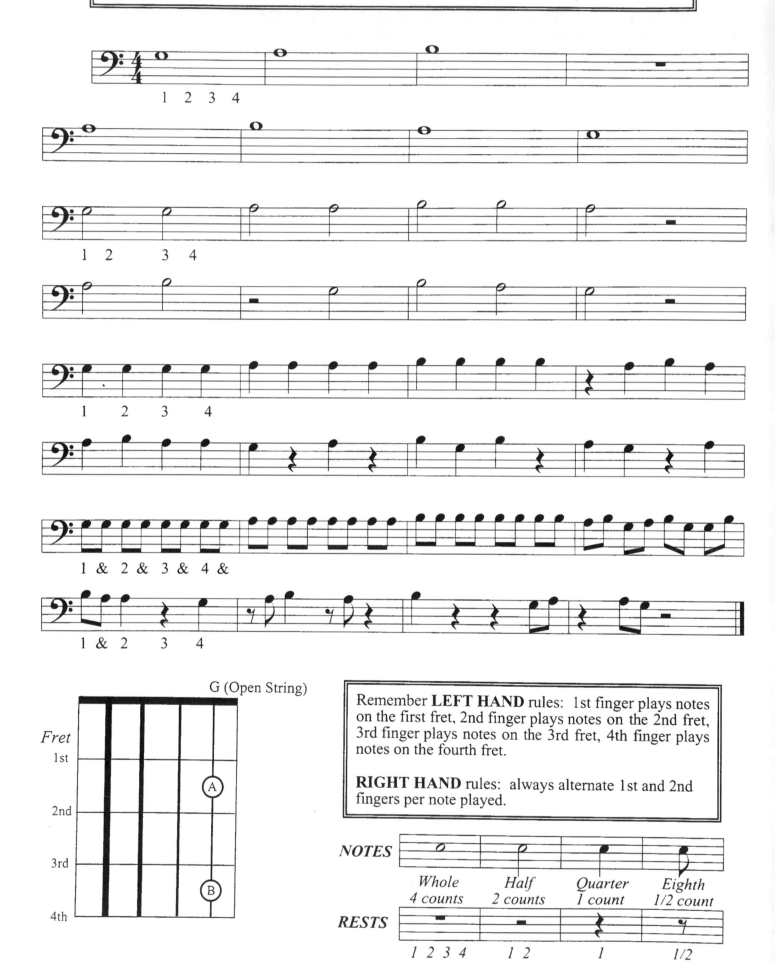

DOTTED NOTE VALUES

A note with a dot placed behind it increases the note's value by half it's regular value.

A dotted half note receives three beats or counts.

1 2 3

A dotted quarter note recieves one and a half beats or counts.

1 2 &

DOTTED NOTES IN THREE-FOUR TIME

The three indicates 3 beats per bar or measure. The four indicates that the **Quarter Note** gets 1 beat or count. This is called a **3/4 TIME SIGNATURE.**

DOTTED NOTES IN FOUR-FOUR TIME

The four on top indicates 4 beats per bar or measure. The four beneath it indicates that the **Quarter Note** gets 1 beat or count. This is called a **4/4 TIME SIGNATURE.**

THE TIE

The **TIE** is a line that connects another note of the same pitch. The first note is struck and held for the time duration of both the first and second or tied note. **DO NOT** strike the second note, let it ring through it's value.

Tie

TIEING IT ALTOGETHER

The exercise below incorporates **DOTTED TIES** and regular **TIES** over 3/4 time. Notice the ties at the end of bars that sustain into following bars.

SIXTEENTH NOTES

It takes four **SIXTEENTH NOTES** to equal one beat or quarter note. These types of notes divide one beat into quarter fractions of count. One sixteenth note has two flags attached to it's stem.

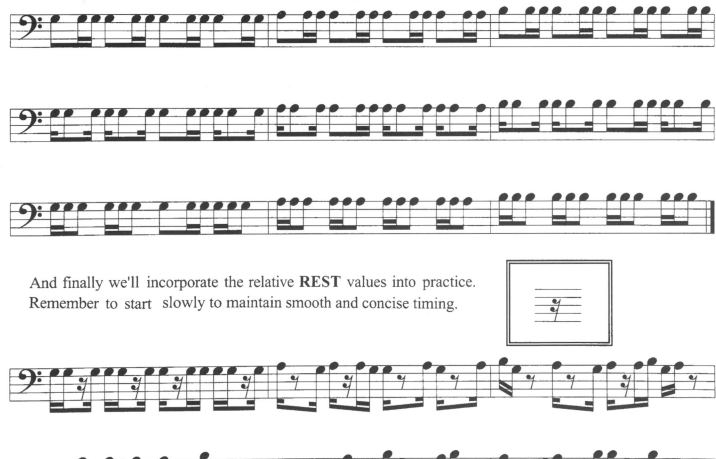

Sometimes a group of **SIXTEENTH NOTES** may be combined with **EIGHT NOTES** and vice versa. The best way to count these subgroups of beats is by the smaller denomination, the sixteenth note method.

And finally we'll incorporate the relative **REST** values into practice. Remember to start slowly to maintain smooth and concise timing.

11

TRIPLET RHYTHMS

A **TRIPLET** is a group of three notes played over the same beat or beats of time as two of it's own regular value. Therefore the **EIGHTH NOTE TRIPLET** would be three eighth notes played over the same count as two eighth notes also known as a polyrythm.

A **QUARTER NOTE TRIPLET** would be three quarter notes played over the same time as two quarter notes.

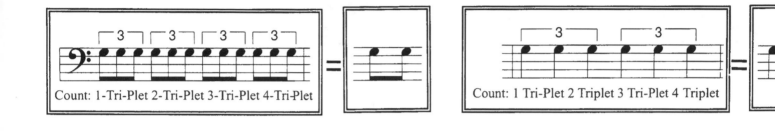

Count: 1-Tri-Plet 2-Tri-Plet 3-Tri-Plet 4-Tri-Plet   Count: 1 Tri-Plet 2 Triplet 3 Tri-Plet 4 Triplet

2nd String Studies
D String Exercise (Notes D, E, and F)

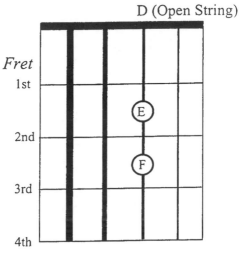

D (Open String)

Remember **LEFT HAND** rules: 1st finger plays notes on the first fret, 2nd finger plays notes on the 2nd fret, 3rd finger plays notes on the 3rd fret, 4th finger plays notes on the fourth fret.

RIGHT HAND rules: always alternate 1st and 2nd fingers per note played.

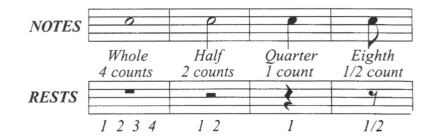

NOTES	Whole *4 counts*	Half *2 counts*	Quarter *1 count*	Eighth *1/2 count*
RESTS				
	1 2 3 4	*1 2*	*1*	*1/2*

DOTTED NOTE VALUES

A note with a dot placed behind it increases the note's value by half it's regular value.

A dotted half note receives three beats or counts.

1 2 3

A dotted quarter note recieves one and a half beats or counts.

1 2 &

DOTTED NOTES IN THREE-FOUR TIME

The three indicates 3 beats per bar or measure. The four indicates that the **Quarter Note** gets 1 beat or count. This is called a **3/4 TIME SIGNATURE.**

DOTTED NOTES IN FOUR-FOUR TIME

The four on top indicates 4 beats per bar or measure. The four beneath it indicates that the **Quarter Note** gets 1 beat or count. This is called a **4/4 TIME SIGNATURE.**

THE TIE

The **TIE** is a line that connects another note of the same pitch. The first note is struck and held for the time duration of both the first and second or tied note. **DO NOT** strike the second note, let it ring through it's value.

TIEING IT ALTOGETHER

The exercise below incorporates **DOTTED TIES** and regular **TIES** over 3/4 time. Notice the ties at the end of bars that sustain into following bars.

15

SIXTEENTH NOTES

It takes four **SIXTEENTH NOTES** to equal one beat or quarter note. These types of notes divide one beat into quarter fractions of count. One sixteenth note has two flags attached to it's stem.

Sometimes a group of **SIXTEENTH NOTES** may be combined with **EIGHT NOTES** and vice versa. The best way to count these subgroups of beats is by the smaller denomination, the sixteenth note method.

And finally we'll incorporate the relative **REST** values into practice. Remember to start slowly to maintain smooth and concise timing.

TRIPLET RHYTHMS

A **TRIPLET** is a group of three notes played over the same beat or beats of time as two of it's own regular value. Therefore the **EIGHTH NOTE TRIPLET** would be three eighth notes played over the same count as two eighth notes also known as a polyrythm.

A **QUARTER NOTE TRIPLET** would be three quarter notes played over the same time as two quarter notes.

Count: 1-Tri-Plet 2-Tri-Plet 3-Tri-Plet 4-Tri-Plet

Count: 1 Tri-Plet 2 Triplet 3 Tri-Plet 4 Triplet

COMBOS ON 1ST AND 2ND STRINGS

3rd String Studies
A String Exercise (Notes A, B, and C)

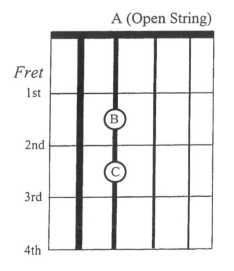

A (Open String)

Fret
1st
2nd
3rd
4th

B

C

Remember **LEFT HAND** rules: 1st finger plays notes on the first fret, 2nd finger plays notes on the 2nd fret, 3rd finger plays notes on the 3rd fret, 4th finger plays notes on the fourth fret.

RIGHT HAND rules: always alternate 1st and 2nd fingers per note played.

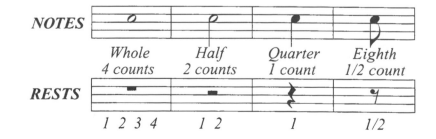

NOTES			
Whole 4 counts	Half 2 counts	Quarter 1 count	Eighth 1/2 count

RESTS			
1 2 3 4	1 2	1	1/2

DOTTED NOTE VALUES

A note with a dot placed behind it increases the note's value by half it's regular value.

A dotted half note receives three beats or counts.

1 2 3

A dotted quarter note recieves one and a half beats or counts.

1 2 &

DOTTED NOTES IN THREE-FOUR TIME

The three indicates 3 beats per bar or measure. The four indicates that the **Quarter Note** gets 1 beat or count. This is called a **3/4 TIME SIGNATURE**.

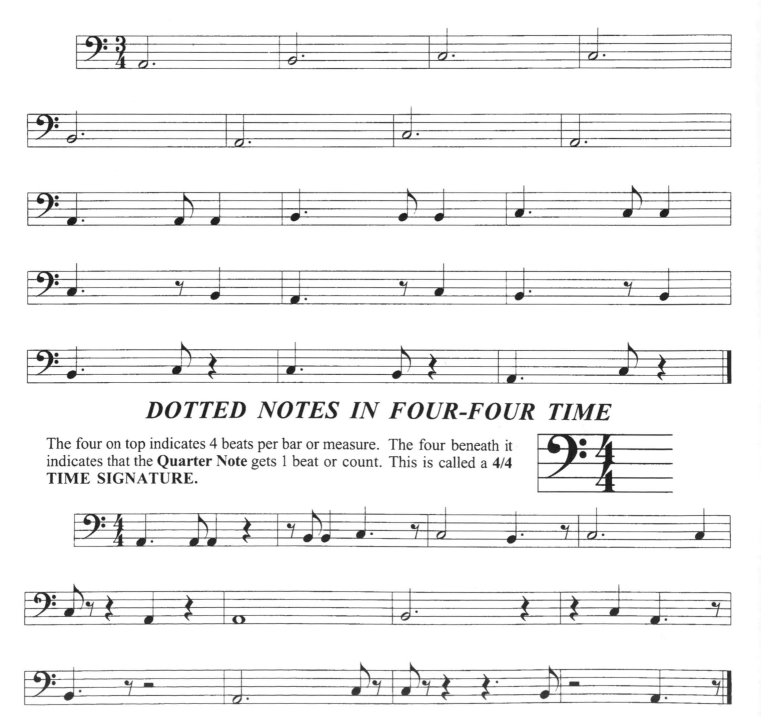

DOTTED NOTES IN FOUR-FOUR TIME

The four on top indicates 4 beats per bar or measure. The four beneath it indicates that the **Quarter Note** gets 1 beat or count. This is called a **4/4 TIME SIGNATURE**.

The **TIE** is a line that connects another note of the same pitch. The first note is struck and held for the time duration of both the first and second or tied note. **DO NOT** strike the second note, let it ring through it's value.

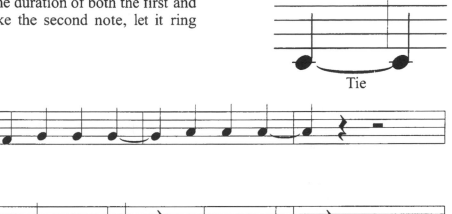

TIEING IT ALTOGETHER

The exercise below incorporates **DOTTED TIES** and regular **TIES** over 3/4 time. Notice the ties at the end of bars that sustain into following bars.

SIXTEENTH NOTES

It takes four **SIXTEENTH NOTES** to equal one beat or quarter note. These types of notes divide one beat into quarter fractions of count. One sixteenth note has two flags attached to it's stem.

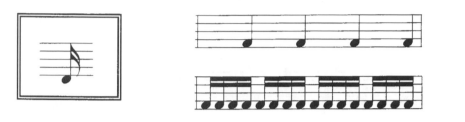

Sometimes a group of **SIXTEENTH NOTES** may be combined with **EIGHT NOTES** and vice versa. The best way to count these subgroups of beats is by the smaller denomination, the sixteenth note method.

And finally we'll incorporate the relative **REST** values into practice. Remember to start slowly to maintain smooth and concise timing.

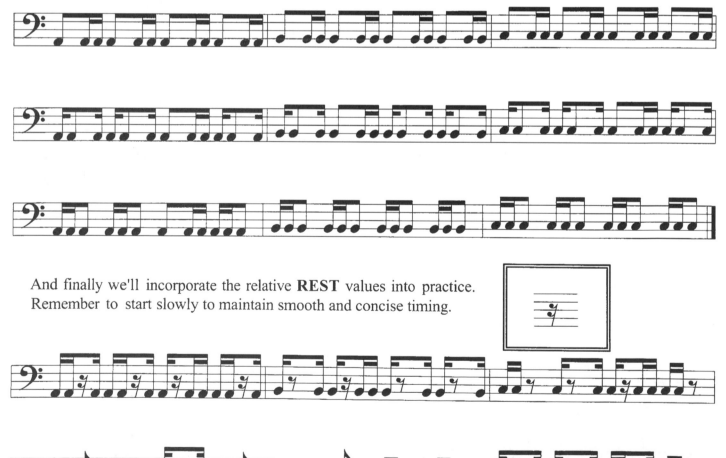

TRIPLET RHYTHMS

A **TRIPLET** is a group of three notes played over the same beat or beats of time as two of it's own regular value. Therefore the **EIGHTH NOTE TRIPLET** would be three eighth notes played over the same count as two eighth notes also known as a polyrythm.

A **QUARTER NOTE TRIPLET** would be three quarter notes played over the same time as two quarter notes.

4th String Studies
E String Exercise (Notes E, F, and G)

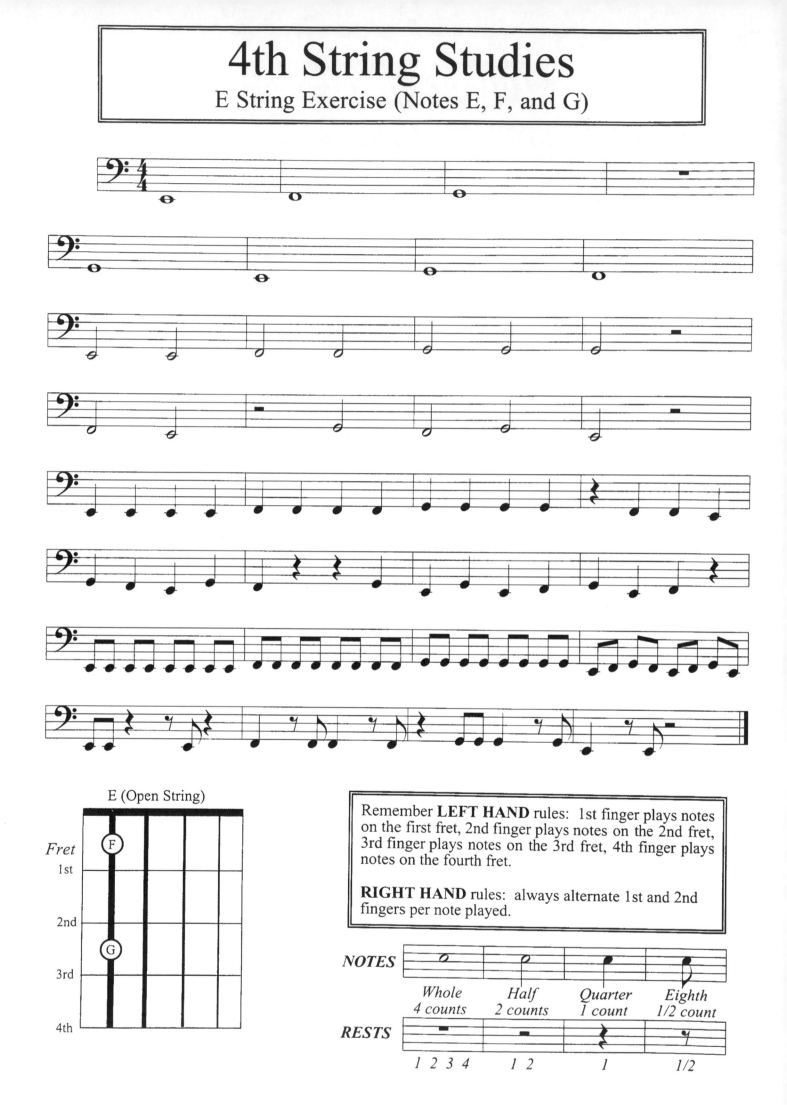

E (Open String)

Remember **LEFT HAND** rules: 1st finger plays notes on the first fret, 2nd finger plays notes on the 2nd fret, 3rd finger plays notes on the 3rd fret, 4th finger plays notes on the fourth fret.

RIGHT HAND rules: always alternate 1st and 2nd fingers per note played.

NOTES			
Whole 4 counts	Half 2 counts	Quarter 1 count	Eighth 1/2 count

RESTS			
1 2 3 4	1 2	1	1/2

DOTTED NOTE VALUES

A note with a dot placed behind it increases the note's value by half it's regular value.

A dotted half note receives three beats or counts.

1 2 3

A dotted quarter note recieves one and a half beats or counts.

1 2 &

DOTTED NOTES IN THREE-FOUR TIME

The three indicates 3 beats per bar or measure. The four indicates that the **Quarter Note** gets 1 beat or count. This is called a **3/4 TIME SIGNATURE.**

DOTTED NOTES IN FOUR-FOUR TIME

The four on top indicates 4 beats per bar or measure. The four beneath it indicates that the **Quarter Note** gets 1 beat or count. This is called a **4/4 TIME SIGNATURE.**

THE TIE

The **TIE** is a line that connects another note of the same pitch. The first note is struck and held for the time duration of both the first and second or tied note. **DO NOT** strike the second note, let it ring through it's value.

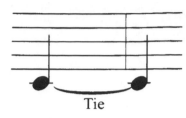

Tie

TIEING IT ALTOGETHER

The exercise below incorporates **DOTTED TIES** and regular **TIES** over 3/4 time. Notice the ties at the end of bars that sustain into following bars.

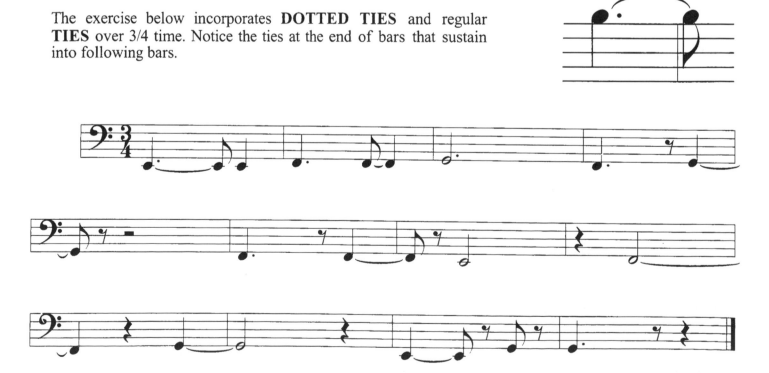

SIXTEENTH NOTES

It takes four **SIXTEENTH NOTES** to equal one beat or quarter note. These types of notes divide one beat into quarter fractions of count. One sixteenth note has two flags attached to it's stem.

Sometimes a group of **SIXTEENTH NOTES** may be combined with **EIGHT NOTES** and vice versa. The best way to count these subgroups of beats is by the smaller denomination, the sixteenth note method.

And finally we'll incorporate the relative **REST** values into practice. Remember to start slowly to maintain smooth and concise timing.

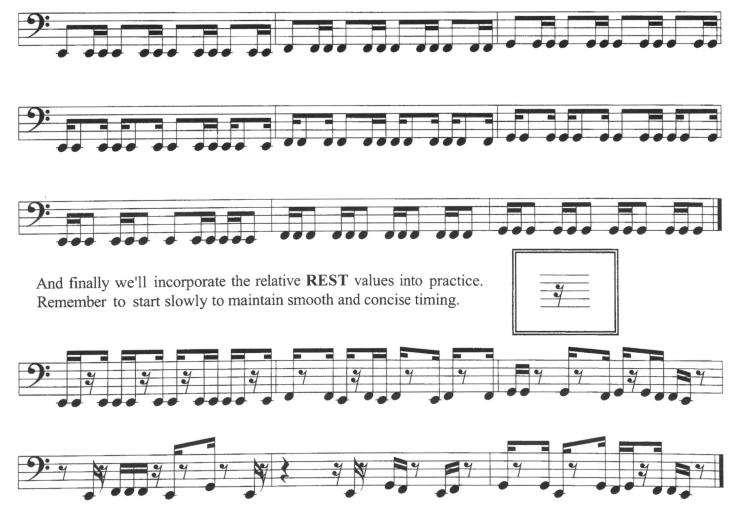

27

TRIPLET RHYTHMS

A **TRIPLET** is a group of three notes played over the same beat or beats of time as two of it's own regular value. Therefore the **EIGHTH NOTE TRIPLET** would be three eighth notes played over the same count as two eighth notes also known as a polyrythm.

A **QUARTER NOTE TRIPLET** would be three quarter notes played over the same time as two quarter notes.

COMBOS ON 3RD AND 4TH STRINGS

COMBOS ON ALL FOURS

30

The Rhythm Gallery

Place your left hand 2nd finger on the C note(3rd string, 3rd fret). Try to get through the entire rhythms notated. As you can see, it starts out very basic and gets more complex, so set your metronome(musical speedometer) at a very slow tempo(suggested 54 beats per min.), and try to play this exercise perfect.

31

Brian Emmel

Introducing:
Sharps, Flats, And Naturals

SYMBOLS:

♯ = **SHARP:** A sharp sign means to play a natural note, i.e. A; one fret higher in pitch(A#).

♭ = **FLAT:** A flat sign means to play a natural note, i.e. A; one fret lower in pitch(Ab).

♮ = **NATURAL:** A natural sign means to return the sharped or flatted note, i.e. A# or Ab;
back to it's original or natural note(A).

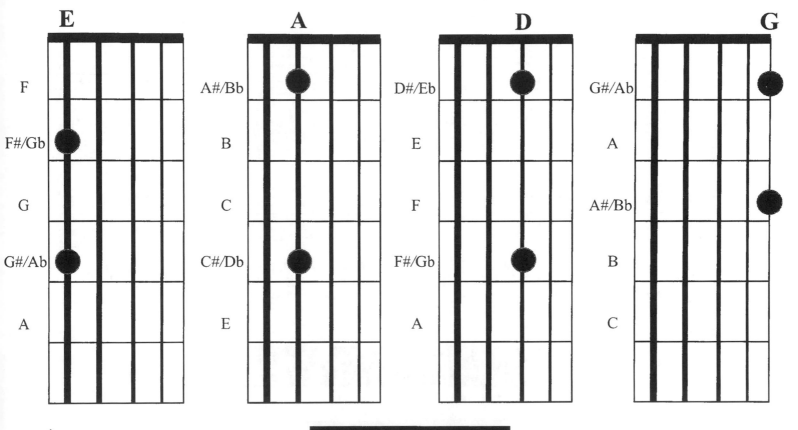

ACCIDENTALS

A sharp or flat note in a measure of music notation means that the note(s) are not found in the KEY SIGNATURE(SEE NEXT CHAPTER). These unrelated notes are called **ACCIDENTALS.**

In this example the G# is the accidental.

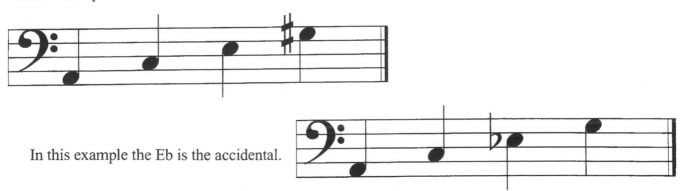

In this example the Eb is the accidental.

Enharmonic Studies

ENHARMONICS are two notes that share the same fret position but have different note names. **EXAMPLE:A#=Bb,G#=Ab,etc.** The following string exercises occure in open through 4th position.This study is to prepare you for **ACCIDENTALS** that may pop up in a piece of music.Remember accidentals are altered notes non related to the specific key.

1ST STRING STUDIES

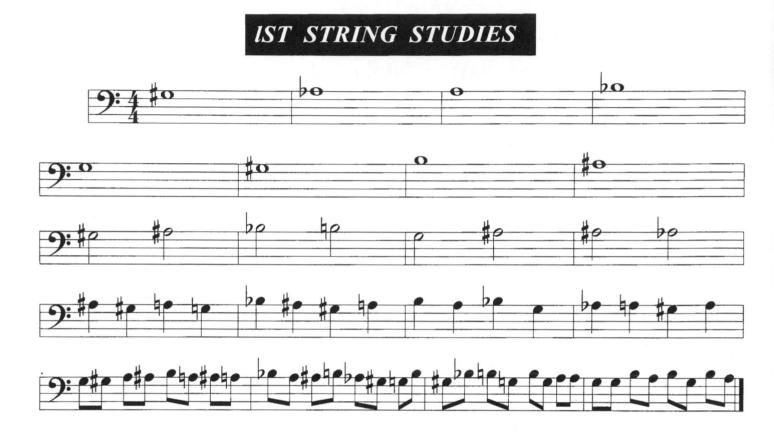

2ND STRING STUDIES

3RD STRING STUDIES

4TH STRING STUDIES

Key Signatures

A key signature is a group of sharps or flats diplayed at the beginning of a piece of music and indicates the notes that get sharped or flatted in the **KEY**. Below are all the **KEY SIGNATURE** headings.

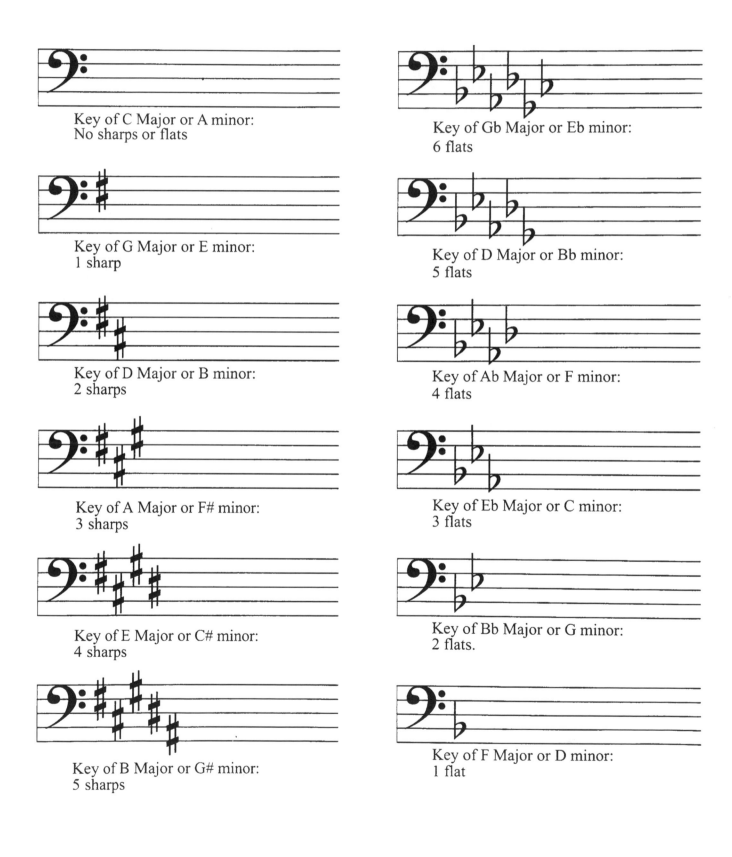

Key of C Major or A minor:
No sharps or flats

Key of Gb Major or Eb minor:
6 flats

Key of G Major or E minor:
1 sharp

Key of D Major or Bb minor:
5 flats

Key of D Major or B minor:
2 sharps

Key of Ab Major or F minor:
4 flats

Key of A Major or F# minor:
3 sharps

Key of Eb Major or C minor:
3 flats

Key of E Major or C# minor:
4 sharps

Key of Bb Major or G minor:
2 flats.

Key of B Major or G# minor:
5 sharps

Key of F Major or D minor:
1 flat

The Major Scale

The Major Scale is the main scale of harmony reference. (do-re-me-fa-so-la-ti-do) is the Major Scale. It's a series of seven notes of the twelve in our musical system, spaced in a series of whole and half step intervals. (whole step=2 frets; half step=1 fret).

	1	2	3	4	5	6	7	8(1)
	do	re	me	fa	so	la	ti	do
WHOLE AND HALF STEPS:	W	W	H	W	W	W	H	
1. C MAJOR SCALE	C	D	E	F	G	A	B	C
2. G MAJOR SCALE	G	A	B	C	D	E	F#	G
3. D MAJOR SCALE	D	E	F#	G	A	B	C#	D
4. A MAJOR SCALE	A	B	C#	D	E	F#	G#	A
5. E MAJOR SCALE	E	F#	G#	A	B	C#	D#	E
6. B MAJOR SCALE	B	C#	D#	E	F#	G#	A#	B
7. F# MAJOR SCALE	F#	G#	A#	B	C#	D#	E#	F#
Gb MAJOR SCALE	Gb	Ab	Bb	Cb	Db	Eb	F	Gb
8. Db MAJOR SCALE	Db	Eb	F	Gb	Ab	Bb	C	Db
9. Ab MAJOR SCALE	Ab	Bb	C	Db	Eb	F	G	Ab
10. Eb MAJOR SCALE	Eb	F	G	Ab	Bb	C	D	Eb
11. Bb MAJOR SCALE	Bb	C	D	Eb	F	G	A	Bb
12. F MAJOR SCALE	F	G	A	Bb	C	D	E	F

Natural Minor Scale

The Natural Minor Scale begins on the 6th tone of each Major Scale.

EXAMPLE:

C MAJOR SCALE: C D E F G A B C
A NATURAL MINOR: A B C D E F G A

Chords And Arpeggios

Bassists must be able to recognize chords and how to play over a piece of music by knowing the notes of each individual chord. This type of reading is called CHORD CHARTS. The bass line should outline the main arrangement of the music or flow with the guitar or piano.

CHORD TYPES

There are four basic chord types: major, minor, dominant(i.e.G7), and diminished.

CHORD CONSTRUCTION

Chords are formed from the major scale. By taking the 1st, 3rd, and 5th notes of the scale we build the TRIAD. By taking the 1st, 3rd, 5th, and 7th(every other note of the scale) we build the 7-TONE chord.

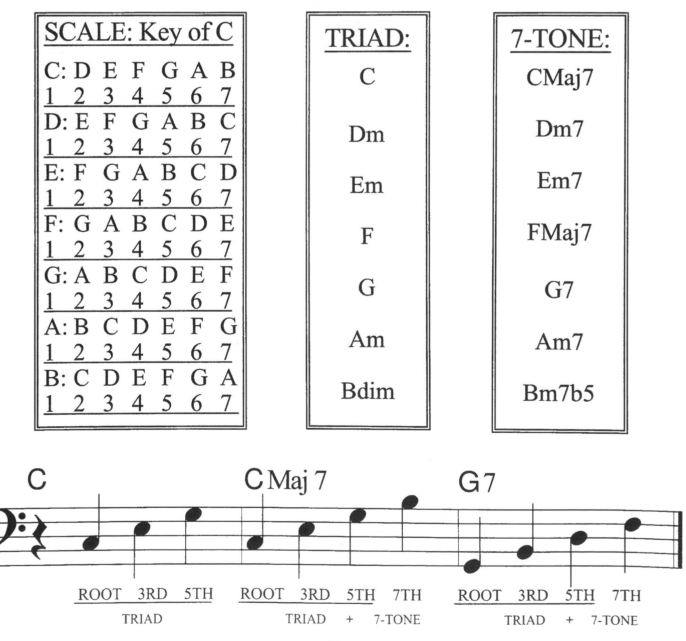

SCALE: Key of C	TRIAD:	7-TONE:
C: D E F G A B 1 2 3 4 5 6 7	C	CMaj7
D: E F G A B C 1 2 3 4 5 6 7	Dm	Dm7
E: F G A B C D 1 2 3 4 5 6 7	Em	Em7
F: G A B C D E 1 2 3 4 5 6 7	F	FMaj7
G: A B C D E F 1 2 3 4 5 6 7	G	G7
A: B C D E F G 1 2 3 4 5 6 7	Am	Am7
B: C D E F G A 1 2 3 4 5 6 7	Bdim	Bm7b5

C

ROOT 3RD 5TH
TRIAD

C Maj 7

ROOT 3RD 5TH 7TH
TRIAD + 7-TONE

G7

ROOT 3RD 5TH 7TH
TRIAD + 7-TONE

Chord Studies In The Key Of C

Exercise 1 contains triads over 3/4 time. Exercise 2 contains seven tone arpeggios over 4/4 or common time. Exercise 3 contains triads over 2/4 or cut time.

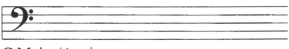

C Major/A minor

Chord Studies In The Key Of G

Exercise 1 contains triads over 3/4 time. Exercise 2 contains seven tone arpeggios over 4/4 or common time. Exercise 3 contains triads over 2/4 or cut time.

G Major/E minor

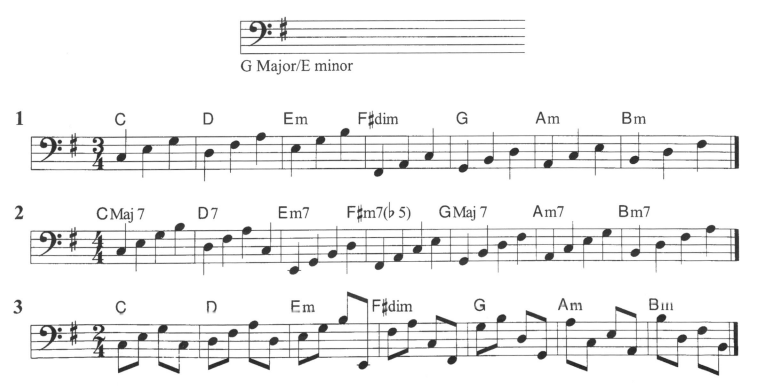

Chord Studies In The Key Of D

Exercise 1 contains triads over 3/4 time. Exercise 2 contains seven tone arpeggios over 4/4 or common time. Exercise 3 contains triads over 2/4 or cut time.

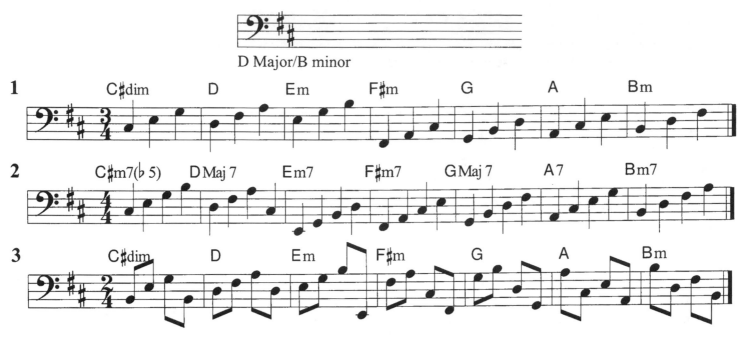

Chord Studies In The Key Of A

Exercise 1 contains triads over 3/4 time. Exercise 2 contains seven tone arpeggios over 4/4 or common time. Exercise 3 contains triads over 2/4 or cut time.

Chord Studies In The Key Of E

Exercise 1 contains triads over 3/4 time. Exercise 2 contains seven tone arpeggios over 4/4 or common time. Exercise 3 contains triads over 2/4 or cut time.

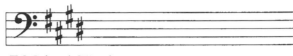

E Major / C# minor

1

2

3

Chord Studies In The Key Of B

Exercise 1 contains triads over 3/4 time. Exercise 2 contains seven tone arpeggios over 4/4 or common time. Exercise 3 contains triads over 2/4 or cut time.

B Major / G# minor

1

C#m · D#m · E

F# · G#m · A#dim · B

2

C#m7 · D#m7 · E Maj 7

F#7 · G#m7 · A#m7(♭5) · B Maj 7

3

C#m · D#m · E

F# · G#m · A#dim · B

Chord Studies In The Key Of Gb

Exercise 1 contains triads over 3/4 time. Exercise 2 contains seven tone arpeggios over 4/4 or common time. Exercise 3 contains triads over 2/4 or cut time.

Gb Major/Eb minor

1

2

3

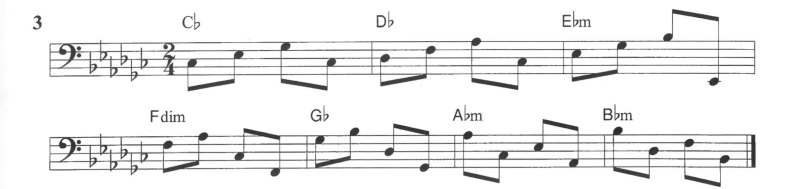

43

Chord Studies In The Key Of Db

Exercise 1 contains triads over 3/4 time. Exercise 2 contains seven tone arpeggios over 4/4 or common time. Exercise 3 contains triads over 2/4 or cut time.

D Major/Bb minor

1

2

3

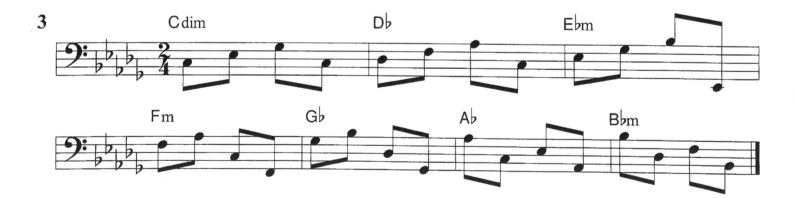

44

Chord Studies In The Key Of Ab

Exercise 1 contains triads over 3/4 time. Exercise 2 contains seven tone arpeggios over 4/4 or common time. Exercise 3 contains triads over 2/4 or cut time.

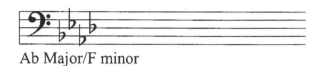

Ab Major/F minor

1

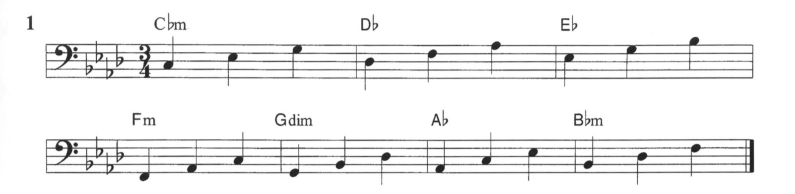

2

3

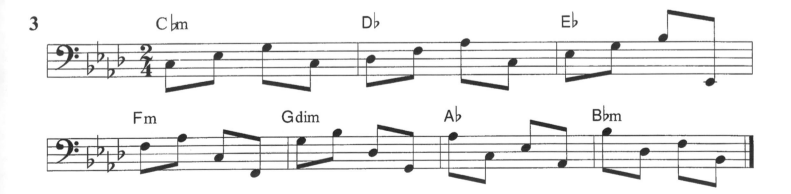

Chord Studies In The Key Of Eb

Exercise 1 contains triads over 3/4 time. Exercise 2 contains seven tone arpeggios over 4/4 or common time. Exercise 3 contains triads over 2/4 or cut time.

Eb Major/C minor

1

2

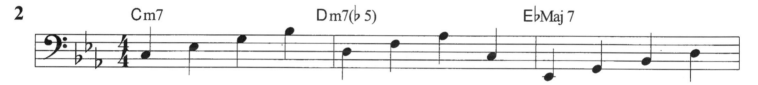

3

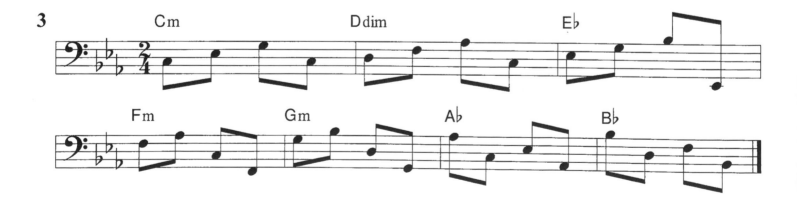

Chord Studies In The Key Of Bb

Exercise 1 contains triads over 3/4 time. Exercise 2 contains seven tone arpeggios over 4/4 or common time. Exercise 3 contains triads over 2/4 or cut time.

Bb Major/G minor

1

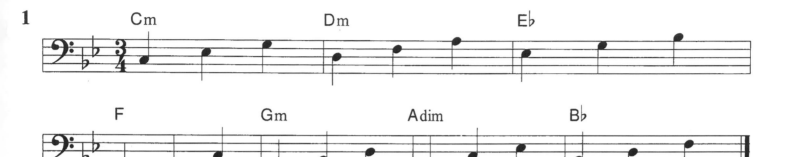

2

3

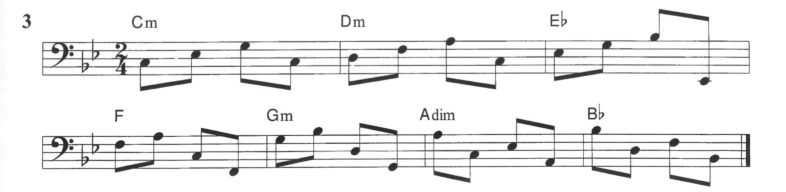

Chord Studies In The Key Of F

Exercise 1 contains triads over 3/4 time. Exercise 2 contains seven tone arpeggios over 4/4 or common time. Exercise 3 contains triads over 2/4 or cut time.

F Major/D minor

1

2

3

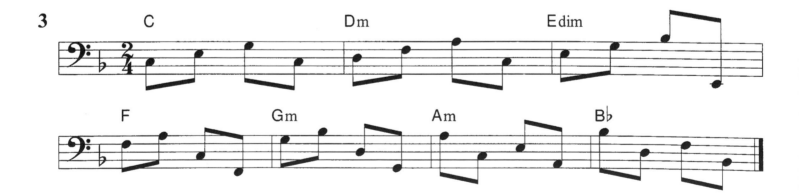

Blues Progressions

The blues, is one of the best forms of music to practice scales, arpeggios, and **PENTATONICS.** There are 3 types of pentatonic scales which play over the basic blues progression I to IV to V.

EXAMPLE: KEY OF C

C MAJOR PENTATONIC = C, D, E, G, A

C MINOR PENTATONIC = C, Eb, F, G, Bb

C BLUES SCALE = C, Eb, F, F#, G, Bb

> The first example shows the use of dotted quarter notes, quarter notes and eighth notes. The I-IV-V is all dominant seven chords, and the bass lines come from the **C MAJOR PENTATONIC.** In measures 11 and 12 are what is known as a **TURN-AROUND,** and is used when returning to the first bar or measure.

The bass lines are constructed from the C Major Scale: C D E F G A B
And the C Major Pentatonic Scale: C D E G A

The same chart now employs the C Blues Scale: C Eb F F# G Bb

This third example employs the identical bass line as example two. The only difference is that the chords are now minor seven chords. In the blues, major and minor chords, and pentatonics can be exchanged over it's key. Experiment with this principle.

Notice how the same bass lines work over the related minor blues key.
Have your teacher play the guitar chords while you play the bass lines.

The bass lines are constructed from the **G Major Scale**: G A B C D E F#
And the G Major Pentatonic Scale: G A B D E

The bass lines are constructed from the G Blues Scale: G Bb C C# D F

50

The following two examples are basic blues progressions in the relative minor keys to **C** and **G**. **A minor** is relative to **C**, and **E minor** is relative to **G**.(The sixth tone in their major scale)

A NATURAL MINOR SCALE = A, B, C, D, E, F, G(The same notes as in the C MAJOR SCALE).

A MINOR PENTATONIC = A, C, D, E, G

A BLUES SCALE = A, C, D, D#, E, G

The bass lines in this example use dotted eighth to sixteenth note rhythms, producing what is known as a **SHUFFLE** type feel in the rhythm.

The walking patterns come out of the A blues scale.

E NATURAL MINOR SCALE = E, F#, G, A, B, C, D(The same notes as in the G MAJOR SCALE).

E MINOR PENTATONIC= E, G, A, B, D

E BLUES SCALE = E, G, A, A#, B, D

The bass lines to this chart came out of the E blues scale.

51

F BLUES

The Sign And The Coda

The **SIGN** is usually placed at the beginning of a piece of music.

The **CODA** is usually placed at the end of a piece of music. It represents the final measures of the music

D.S. AL CODA is a **command** at the end of a measure; telling the player to go back to the **SlGN**, play up to the **command**, then go directly to the final bars of music marked by the **CODA**.

Chord Inversions

A chord symbol such as **G/B** means the standard G chord is to have the note B in the lowest position, or in the ROOT position in place of the G which usually holds the root position. Bass players usually play the B in this example.

53

Congratulations!

You should now have a basic foundation in sight-reading, and understanding rhythm notation. You have also learned chord composition while developing your sight-reading skills. The remaining exercises in this book are for your enjoyment; playing over what is known as **CHORD CHARTS**. Have your teacher play guitar over the charts and exercise your knowledge of chords or arpeggios from the previous chapters in this book. Feel free to improvise over these chord exchanges, using different rhythm variations and incorporate other scale tones in the keys of the charts. Don't forget to first look at each key signature. Good luck! Wang Chung, have fun!

Chord Charts

The / / / / symbolize the number of beats per measure in each chart. Because notation is exempt, you are free to improvise or do whatever you want over each measure.

Leave It To Beavis

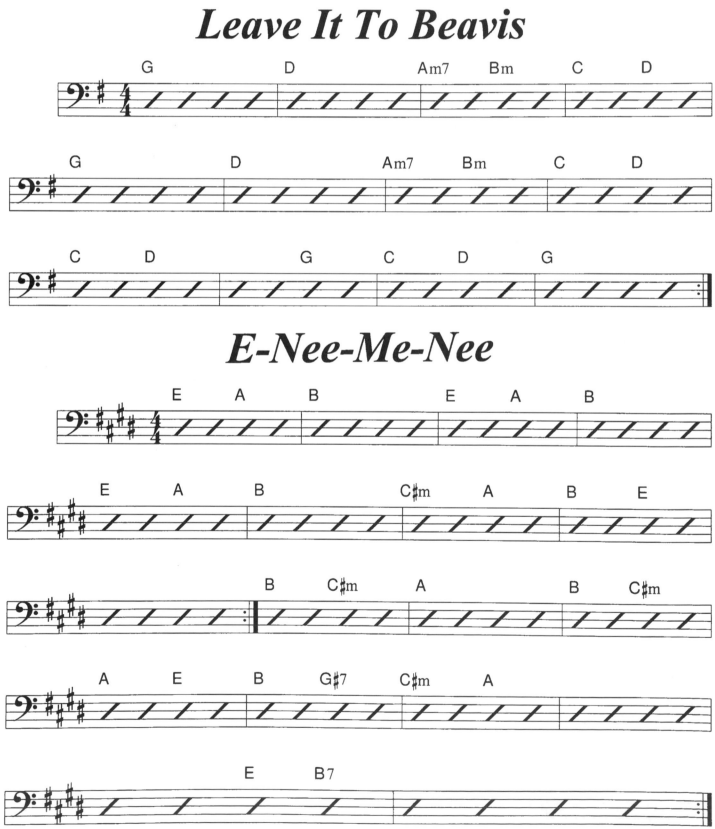

E-Nee-Me-Nee

54

A.D.

More Great Bass Books from Centerstream...

5-STRING BASS METHOD
by Brian Emmel
Besides discussing how to adapt to the differences in the 5-string versus 4-, this book explores the various ways of using the 5-string, practice tips, different techniques, and practical applications for various genres demonstrated through songs on the 37-minute accompanying CD.
00000134 Book/CD Pack...$17.95

ART OF THE SLAP
by Brian Emmel
This slap bass method book, designed for advanced beginning to intermediate bassists, is based on the understanding and application of modes. The focus is on the concept of groove sculpting from modes, and not on actual right- and left-hand techniques. The CD features recordings of all the examples, plus a split-channel option to let you practice your playing. Includes 13 songs.
00000229 Book/CD Pack...$16.95

FENDER PRECISION BASSES
by Detlef Schmidt
Introduced in 1951, the Fender Precision Bass is the precursor of all modern electric basses. This book takes a look at the history of the "slab body basses" and the most famous players. In addition to many historical photos, the full-color book lists many basses with beautiful pictures, detail shots, and anecdotes. This book is a must-have for every bass player and enthusiast or collector.
00001348 Hardcover/160 pages................................$35.00

BEGINNING TO ADVANCED 4-STRING BASS
by Brian Emmel
This instructional video by noted instructor/author Brian Emmel leaves no stone unturned in explaining all there is to know about 4-string bass basics! Designed for the beginning to advanced player, Brian's step-by-step demonstrations form the foundation for understanding music theory and building bass technique. Topics covered range from common musical terminology, to playing in a garage band, to laying down tracks in a recording studio. 60 minutes.
00000374 DVD $19.95

BLUES GROOVES
Traditional Concepts for Playing 4 & 5 String Blues Bass
by Brian Emmel
This book/CD pack has been designed to educate bass enthusiasts about the development of different styles and traditions throughout the history of the blues, from the 1920s to the early 1970s. Players will learn blues scales, rhythm variations, turnarounds, endings and grooves, and styles such as Chicago blues, jazz, Texas blues, rockabilly, R&B and more. The CD includes 36 helpful example tracks.
00000269 Book/CD Pack...$17.95

ULTIMATE BASS EXERCISES
by Max Palermo
Bassist and educator Max Palermo takes you through more than 700 easy, step-by-step exercises for finger building, based on the 24 possible fingering combinations. 158 pages.
00000476...$19.95

BASS GUITAR CHORDS
by Ron Middlebrook
84 of the most popular chords for bass guitar. Covers: finger placement, note construction, chromatic charts, and the most commonly used bass scales. Also has a helpful explanation of the common 2-5-1 progression, and the chords in all keys.
00000073...$2.95

HIP-HOP GROOVES FOR BASS
by Max Palermo
From the irresistible party jams of South Bronx to the urban sounds of today, hip-hop has maintained close links with its roots. Many of its characteristic sounds and beats come from funk, soul, and R&B origins. The electric bass plays a key role in creating the groovin' that gives hip-hop a unique, attractive feel. This book/CD set contains 90 authentic hip-hop licks that will lead you to the vibrant world of hip-hop style. All the bass lines are demonstrated on the CD's full-performance tracks and transcribed in standard notation and tablature. Jamming along with these patterns, you will improve your technique while you learn how to lay down the right groove. Just listen to the tracks and concentrate on playing with a good-time feel. Enjoy!
00001174...$14.95

CENTERSTREAM

P.O. Box 17878 - Anaheim Hills, CA 92817
(714) 779-9390   centerstrm@aol.com | www.centerstream-usa.com